THE REBEL'S SILHOUETTE

FAIZ AHMED FAIZ

THE REBEL'S SILHOUETTE

translated by
AGHA SHAHID ALI

PEREGRINE SMITH BOOKS
SALT LAKE CITY

First edition
95 94 93 92 91 5 4 3 2 1
Copyright 1991 by Agha Shahid Ali

Published by Gibbs Smith, Publisher, Peregrine Smith Books, P.O. Box 667,
Layton, Utah 84041 (801) 544-9800

Cover Design by Randall Smith Associates
Typography by Design Type Service
Original Urdu calligraphy by
   S.M. Mazhar of Maktaba Jamia, Ltd., New Delhi

Printed and bound in the United States of America

Library of Congress Catalog-in-Publication Data

Faiz, Faiz Ahmed, 1911-
   [Selections. English. 1991]
   The rebel's silhouette / Faiz Ahmed Faiz; translated by Agha Shahid Ali.
      p.   cm.—(The Peregrine Smith poetry series)
   ISBN 0-87905-378-X
   I. Agha, Shahid Ali, 1949- . II. Title.   III. Series
PK2199.F255A6   1991
891'.43917—dc20   90-22138
                                                                      CIP

Translator's Dedication

For Paru

Preface

SALMAN RUSHDIE in *Shame:* "Omar Khayyam's position as a poet is curious. He was never very popular in his native Persia; and he exists in the West in a translation that is really a complete reworking of his verses, in many cases very different from the spirit (to say nothing of the content) of the original. . . . It is generally believed that something is always lost in translation; I cling to the notion—and use, in evidence, the success of Fitzgerald-Khayyam—that something can also be gained."

Faiz Ahmed Faiz, of course, is a very popular poet in the Indian subcontinent, lionized by the literary elite as well as the masses. To have to introduce him is frustrating because he should already be familiar to poets and poetasters all over the world; a non-subcontinental audience, however, may begin to understand his stature as a poet *and* public figure by imagining a combination of Pablo Neruda, Nazim Hikmet, Octavio Paz, and the Palestinian, Mahmoud Darwish. Born in Sialkot, in undivided Punjab in 1910, Faiz earned a master's degree in English literature, and another in Arabic literature. During World War II, he served in the Indian Army, obtaining the rank of lieutenant colonel. After independence, which accompanied the partition of the subcontinent (1947), Faiz chose to live in Pakistan and became editor of *The Pakistan Times*. In 1951, along with several left-wing army officers, he was arrested on the charge of planning a Soviet-sponsored coup; he spent four years in prison, mostly in solitary confinement, under sentence of death, but was released in 1955. He returned to work on *The Pakistan Times*.

In 1958, he was removed from that post when a new military government took over. Interestingly, President Ayub Khan, despite having Faiz jailed briefly, mentioned him first when UNESCO was approaching various governments to nominate *the* representative writers of their countries for the purpose of translating them into other languages. Faiz had truly become a public figure. After translations of his work appeared in Russian, he was awarded the Lenin Peace Prize in 1962. When Zulfikar Ali Bhutto became Prime Minister, Faiz was appointed chair of the National Council on the Arts, a position he lost when Bhutto was overthrown by Zia ul-Haq. After that, Faiz lived in exile in Beirut—till the Israeli invasion of 1982—and edited *Lotus,* the journal of the Afro-Asian Writers' Association. He died in Lahore in November 1984, an event that was reported, sometimes in banner headlines, in the first pages of newspapers in India, Pakistan, the Soviet Union, and throughout the Middle East.

Given Faiz's political commitments, particularly his Marxist understanding of history, audiences may hastily assume that he was a poet of slogans. Faiz's genius, however, lay in his ability to balance his politics with his (in some ways stringently traditional) aesthetics without compromising either. He once advised a poet to avoid didactic and rhetorical gestures. He also said that "the future of the *ghazal,* like the future of all poetry, depends above all on the talent of its future practitioners. Pedantically speaking, there is nothing good or bad in any poetic form, but that the poet makes it so." Faiz was such a master of the *ghazal,* a form that predates Chaucer, that he transformed its every stock image and, as if by magic, brought absolutely new associations into being. For example, the Beloved—an archetypal figure in Urdu poetry—can mean friend, woman, God. Faiz not only tapped into those meanings, but extended them to include the Revolution. Waiting for the Revolution can be as intoxicating as waiting for one's lover.

Here it may be useful to explain the form of the *ghazal.* Composed of thematically autonomous couplets that are linked together in a strict scheme of rhyme and meter, the *ghazal,* in its first couplet, establishes a scheme that occurs in both lines. As John Hollander says, "For couplets, the ghazal is prime; at the end / Of each one's a refrain like a chime: *'at the end.' "* Having seen this couplet, the reader would know that the second line of every succeeding couplet would end with "at the end," the phrase preceded by a word or syllable rhyming with prime and chime. Thus Hollander continues: "But in subsequent couplets throughout the whole poem, / It's the second line only will rhyme at the end." The reason this form is so tantalizing is that it gives the poet the freedom to engage with all kinds of themes, issues, attitudes, while keeping him gratefully shackled. Thus one couplet may be political, another religious, another romantic, and so on. A *ghazal* must have at least four couplets; there is no maximum limit. Let me offer one more couplet from Hollander: "You gathered all manner of flowers all day, / But your hands were most fragrant of thyme, at the end." Because translating a *ghazal* is just about impossible, I have adopted loose, free verse stanzas to suggest the elliptical complexities and power of Faiz's couplets. Obviously, the magic of the form is missing.

In Faiz's poetry, suffering is seldom, perhaps never, private (in the sense the suffering of confessional poets is). Though deeply personal, it is almost never isolated from a sense of history and injustice. In a very famous poem, "Don't Ask Me For That Love Again," Faiz breaks from Urdu's traditional way of looking at the Beloved. Not only does he refuse to despair but, in a radical departure from convention, asks the Beloved—even while acknowledging her immense importance—to accept his social commitment as more important than their love. This was a revolutionary poem, envied by many Urdu poets who wished they had first broken from the tradition in which everything was either the Beloved or nothing. Faiz did not discard the tradition: the poem clearly established the importance of the Beloved and her beauty. But it does some plain speaking (almost like Cordelia to Lear), granting love its due, but no more. That Faiz had emphasized political commitment here did not of course, mean that he would not, in other poems, address the Beloved in the traditional manner, showing how the speaker's life depended entirely on her. But then often, when he addresses the Beloved, he is also addressing a figure that, depending on the context, may very well be the Revolution—Revolution as a lost lover, or a cruel lover refusing to return.

In "Don't Ask Me For That Love Again," Faiz draws a line of demarcation between the political and the romantic. But many times, a mingling of the political and the romantic pervades his poetry. Sometimes the two, especially in the *ghazals,* are entangled in such a way that there is no point in trying to separate them: the political meaning informs the romantic and the romantic, the political. Nevertheless, Faiz, a man who was jailed for his beliefs, certainly does have poems, many in fact, that are exclusively political. Among them one can list the Bangladesh poems, as well as *"You* Tell Us What To Do." And then Faiz has political poems that are not direct; instead, they are richly symbolic. And the fact that they are symbolic is sometimes, in itself, a political statement. Indeed, Urdu has a long enough tradition of concealing politics in symbols. In nineteenth-century Urdu poetry, the stock figure of the Executioner often represented the British (a way of dodging the censors as well as the gallows: in the summer of 1857, the British had hanged almost thirty thousand people from the trees of Delhi to terrorize the population and punish it for what is often called the Mutiny). In Pakistan, under the censorship of various military dictatorships, it was often impossible to name things exactly.

I have undertaken my translations in the hope that something may be borne across to English readers. This book is not for purists, because at times I have had no choice but to adjust, especially in the *ghazals,* the letter of Faiz's work—a letter to which I have an emotional, even a sentimental, attachment, but only in the original Urdu. If my translations manage to convey some of Faiz's magic and a fraction of the complexity that resulted from his political and cultural background, I would consider myself as having managed to pay a modest tribute to his immense humanity.

About the Title

Though the poems here are taken from various Faiz volumes, for my selection (which is arranged chronologically) I have chosen to adapt the title of his first volume, *Naqsh-e-Faryādī (Sketch of the Plaintiff* or *Outline of the Plaintiff* or *Features of the Plaintiff)*—a phrasing that captures the spirit of his entire output. However, because Faiz does not recognize the moral authority of man-made courts, he is a plaintiff only in the courts of the universe. Clearly, a rebel.

Acknowledgments

These translations, in one form or another, have appeared in *Chandrabhaga, Delos, Denver Quarterly, Graham House Review, Grand Street, The Greenfield Review, Kayak, The Literary Review, The New Renaissance, Nimrod, Paintbrush, Poetry East, Quarterly West, Sonora Review, Stone Country,* and *Willow Springs.*

A fellowship from the Ingram Merrill Foundation and a summer grant from Hamilton College helped me substantially in finishing these translations. I also thank Sufia Agha Ashraf Ali for her help during the summers of 1988 and 1989 in Kashmir.

Contents

THE REBEL'S SILHOUETTE

اشعار

رات یوں دل میں تری کھوئی ہوئی یاد آئی

جیسے ویرانے میں چپکے سے بہار آجائے

جیسے صحراؤں میں ہولے سے چلے بادِ نسیم

جیسے بیمار کو بے وجہ قرار آجائے

Last Night

At night my lost memory of you returned

and I was like the empty field where springtime,
without being noticed, is bringing flowers;

I was like the desert over which
the breeze moves gently, with great care;

I was like the dying patient
who, for no reason, smiles.

مجھ سے پہلی سی محبت مری محبوب نہ مانگ

مجھ سے پہلی سی محبت مری محبوب نہ مانگ

میں نے سمجھا تھا کہ تو ہے تو درخشاں ہے حیات

تیرا غم ہے تو غمِ دہر کا جھگڑا کیا ہے

تیری صورت سے ہے عالم میں بہاروں کو ثبات

تیری آنکھوں کے سوا دنیا میں رکھا کیا ہے؟

تو جو مل جائے تو تقدیر نگوں ہو جائے

یوں نہ تھا میں نے فقط چاہا تھا یوں ہو جائے

اور بھی دکھ ہیں زمانے میں محبت کے سوا

راحتیں اور بھی ہیں وصل کی راحت کے سوا

ان گنت صدیوں کے تاریک بہیمانہ طلسم

ریشم و اطلس و کمخواب میں بنوائے ہوئے

جا بجا بکتے ہوئے کوچہ و بازار میں جسم

خاک میں لتھڑے ہوئے خون میں نہلائے ہوئے

لوٹ جاتی ہے ادھر کو بھی نظر کیا کیجے

اب بھی دلکش ہے ترا حسن، مگر کیا کیجے

اور بھی دکھ ہیں زمانے میں محبت کے سوا

راحتیں اور بھی ہیں وصل کی راحت کے سوا

مجھ سے پہلی سی محبت مری محبوب نہ مانگ

4

Don't Ask Me for that Love Again

That which then was ours, my love,
don't ask me for that love again.
The world then was gold, burnished with light—
and only because of you. That's what I had believed.
How could one weep for sorrows other than yours?
How could one have any sorrow but the one you gave?
So what were these protests, these rumors of injustice?
A glimpse of your face was evidence of springtime.
The sky, wherever I looked, was nothing but your eyes.
If you'd fall into my arms, Fate would be helpless.

All this I'd thought, all this I'd believed.
But there were other sorrows, comforts other than love.
The rich had cast their spell on history:
dark centuries had been embroidered on brocades and silks.
Bitter threads began to unravel before me
as I went into alleys and in open markets
saw bodies plastered with ash, bathed in blood.
I saw them sold and bought, again and again.
This too deserves attention. I can't help but look back
when I return from those alleys—what should one do?
And you still are so ravishing—what should I do?
There are other sorrows in this world,
comforts other than love.
Don't ask me, my love, for that love again.

دونوں جہان تیری محبت میں ہار کے
وہ جا رہا ہے کوئی شبِ غم گزار کے

ویراں ہے میکدہ، خم و ساغر اُداس ہیں
تم کیا گئے کہ روٹھ گئے دن بہار کے

اک فرصتِ گناہ ملی، وہ بھی چار دن
دیکھے ہیں ہم نے حوصلے پروردگار کے

دنیا نے تیری یاد سے بیگانہ کر دیا
تجھ سے بھی دلفریب ہیں غم روزگار کے

بھولے سے مسکرا تو دیئے تھے وہ آج فیض
مت پوچھ ولولے دلِ ناکردہ کار کے

Ghazal

He bet both this life and the next
and gambled all night for your love
he first lost earth then eternity
    Now he departs from his night of grief
    defeat visible in his eyes

Oh what a desolation
the taverns deserted each glass disconsolate
    Love when you left
    even springtime forsook me
    you left and that season disowned this world

You made it so brief our time on earth
its exquisite sins this sensation Oh Almighty
of forgetting you
    We know how vulnerable you are
    we know you are a coward God

This rapture of simple routines life's common struggles
have surpassed my memory of love
    It's proved more enticing just to survive
    even more than you
    my love

Today she forgot herself her usual ways
her face broke as if by chance
into a smile
    Don't ask what happened to the defeated heart
    Oh Faiz how it broke once again
    into hopeless longing

تنہائی

پھر کوئی آیا دلِ زار! نہیں کوئی نہیں
راہرو ہوگا، کہیں اور چلا جائے گا
ڈھل چکی رات، بکھرنے لگا تاروں کا غبار
لڑکھڑانے لگے ایوانوں میں خوابیدہ چراغ
سو گئی راستہ تک تک کے ہر اک راہگزار
اجنبی خاک نے دھندلا ئے قدموں کے سراغ
گل کرو شمعیں، بڑھا دو مے و مینا و ایاغ
اپنے بے خواب کواڑوں کو مقفل کر لو
اب یہاں کوئی نہیں، کوئی نہیں آئے گا

Solitude

Someone, finally, is here! No, unhappy heart, no one—
just a passerby on his way.
The night has surrendered
to clouds of scattered stars.
The lamps in the halls waver.
Having listened with longing for steps,
the roads too are asleep.
A strange dust has buried every footprint.

Blow out the lamps, break the glasses, erase
all memory of wine. Heart,
bolt forever your sleepless doors,
tell every dream that knocks to go away.
No one, now no one will ever return.

تم آئے ہو' نہ شبِ انتظار گزری ہے
تلاش میں ہے سحر' بار بار گزری ہے

جنوں میں جتنی بھی گزری' بکار گزری ہے
اگرچہ دل پہ خرابی ہزار گزری ہے

ہوئی ہے حضرتِ ناصح سے گفتگو جس شب
وہ شب ضرور سرِ کوئے یار گزری ہے

نہ گل کھلے ہیں' نہ اُن سے ملے' نہ پی ہے
عجیب رنگ میں اب کے بہار گزری ہے

چمن میں غارتِ گلچیں سے جانے کیا گزری
قفس سے آج صبا بے قرار گزری ہے

Ghazal

You haven't come
I've spent the night waiting
    The dawn is in search
    It passes this way again and again

Whatever I bore in the madness of rapture
has proved useful
    though the heart's been made useless
    broken a thousand times

The evening I must listen
to words of caution
from the wise
    That night without fail
    I'm in my lover's arms

There are no blossoms
there is no lover
and no wine
    In what strange manner
    has spring come this time?

Who knows
what was the garden's grief
when it saw its flowers crushed to nothing?
    This was seen: when dawn came
    the breeze passed
    a restless wind through the cages

دل میں اب یوں ترے بھولے ہوئے غم آتے ہیں

جیسے بچھڑے ہوئے کعبے میں صنم آتے ہیں

ایک اک کر کے ہوئے جاتے ہیں تارے روشن

میری منزل کی طرف تیرے قدم آتے ہیں

رقص مے تیز کرو، ساز کی لے تیز کرو

سوئے مے خانہ سفیرانِ حرم آتے ہیں

اور کچھ دیر نہ گزرے شبِ فرقت سے کہو

دل بھی کم دُکھتا ہے، وہ یاد بھی کم آتے ہیں

Ghazal

The heart a desecrated temple
    in it all statues of you broken
Those forgotten sorrows
    my memories of you return
    gods abandoned by their worshippers

One by one by one
    the stars light up the sky
In step with them
    you approach me in the dark
    your final destination

Tonight increase the pace
    with which the liquor is poured
    Oh tell the drummer to play a breathless beat
Worshippers have abandoned the mosques
    they're coming here to the wine house

It is the night of waiting
    tell her let no more time elapse
This pain of longing may dull
    already my memory is beginning to blur
    at any moment I may forget her

شفق کی راکھ میں جل بجھ کے گیا ستارۂ ہجوم
شبِ فراق کے گیسو فضا میں لہرائے

کوئی پکارو کہ اک عمر ہونے آئی ہے
فلک کو قافلۂ روز و شام ٹھہرائے

یہ ضد ہے یادِ حریفانِ بادہ پیما کی
کہ شب کو چاند نہ نکلے، نہ دن کو ابر آئے

صبا نے پھر درِ زنداں پہ آکے دی دستک
سحر قریب ہے، دل سے کہو نہ گھبرائے

Ghazal

In the sun's last embers, the evening star burns to ash.
Night draws its curtains, separating lovers.

Won't someone cry out, protest Heaven's tyranny? An era has
      passed,
and Time is still stranded, its caravan of day and night lost.

Nostalgia for friends and wine: to crush that sorrow,
we'll allow memory nothing, neither the moon nor the rain.

Once again the breeze knocks on the prison door.
It whispers, Don't give up, wait a little, Dawn is near.

روشن کہیں بہار کے امکاں ہوئے تو ہیں
گلشن میں چاک چند گریباں ہوئے تو ہیں

اب بھی خزاں کا راج ہے لیکن کہیں کہیں
گوشے رہِ چمن میں غزل خواں ہوئے تو ہیں

ٹھہری ہوئی ہے شب کی سیاہی وہیں مگر
کچھ کچھ سحر کے رنگ پرافشاں ہوئے تو ہیں

ان میں لہو جلا ہو ہمارا، کہ جان و دل
محفل میں کچھ چراغ فروزاں ہوئے تو ہیں

ہاں کج کرو کلاہ کہ سب کچھ لٹے کے ہم
اب بے نیازِ گردشِ دوراں ہوئے تو ہیں

اہلِ قفس کی صبحِ چمن میں کھلے گی آنکھ
بادِ صبا سے وعدہ و پیماں ہوئے تو ہیں

ہے دشت اب بھی دشت، مگر خونِ پائے فیض
سیراب اب چند خارِ مغیلاں ہوئے تو ہیں

August 1952

It's still distant, but there are hints of springtime:
some flowers, aching to bloom, have torn open their collars.

In this era of autumn, almost winter, leaves can still be heard:
their dry orchestras play, hidden in corners of the garden.

Night is still where it was, but colors at times take flight,
leaving red feathers of dawn on the sky.

Don't regret our breath's use as air, our blood's as oil—
some lamps at last are burning in the night.

Tilt your cup, don't hesitate! Having given up all,
we don't need wine. We've freed ourselves, made Time irrelevant.

When imprisoned man opens his eyes, cages will dissolve: air, fire,
water, earth—all have pledged such dawns, such gardens to him.

Your feet bleed, Faiz, something surely will bloom
as you water the desert simply by walking through it.

زنداں کی ایک شام

شام کے پیچ و خم ستاروں سے
زینہ زینہ اُتر رہی ہے رات
یوں صبا پاس سے گزرتی ہے
جیسے کہہ دی کسی نے پیار کی بات
صحنِ زنداں کے بے وطن اشجار
سرنگوں، محو ہیں بنانے میں
دامنِ آسماں پہ نقش و نگار
شانۂ بام پر دمکتا ہے!
مہرباں چاندنی کا دستِ جمیل
خاک میں گھل گئی ہے آبِ نجوم
نور میں گھل گیا ہے عرش کا نیل
سبز گوشوں میں نیلگوں سائے
لہلہاتے ہیں جس طرح دل میں
موجِ دردِ فراقِ یار آئے
دل سے پیہم خیال کہتا ہے
اتنی شیریں ہے زندگی اس پل
ظلم کا زہر گھولنے والے
کامراں ہو سکیں گے آج نہ کل
جلوہ گاہِ وصال کی شمعیں
وہ بجھا بھی چکے اگر تو کیا
چاند کو گُل کریں تو ہم جانیں

18

A Prison Evening

Each star a rung,
night comes down the spiral
staircase of the evening.
The breeze passes by so very close
as if someone just happened to speak of love.
In the courtyard,
the trees are absorbed refugees
embroidering maps of return on the sky.
On the roof,
the moon—lovingly, generously—
is turning the stars
into a dust of sheen.
From every corner, dark-green shadows,
in ripples, come towards me.
At any moment they may break over me,
like the waves of pain each time I remember
this separation from my lover.

This thought keeps consoling me:
though tyrants may command that lamps be smashed
in rooms where lovers are destined to meet,
they cannot snuff out the moon, so today,
nor tomorrow, no tyranny will succeed,
no poison of torture make me bitter,
if just one evening in prison
can be so strangely sweet,
if just one moment anywhere on this earth.

زنداں کی ایک صبح

رات باقی تھی ابھی جب سرِ بالیں آکر
چاند نے مجھ سے کہا۔ "جاگ سحر آئی ہے
جاگ اِس شب جو مئے خواب ترا حصہ تھی
جام کے لب سے تہِ جام اُتر آئی ہے"
عکس جاناں کو دہ دع کرکے اٹھی میری نظر
شب کے ٹھہرے ہوئے پانی کی سیہ چادر پر

جا بجا رقص میں آنے لگے چاندی کے بھنور
چاند کے ہاتھ سے تاروں کے کنول گر گر کر
ڈوبتے، تیرتے، مرجھاتے رہے، کھلتے رہے
رات اور صبح بہت دیر گلے ملتے رہے

صحنِ زنداں میں رفیقوں کے سنہرے چہرے
سطحِ ظلمت سے دمکتے ہوئے اُبھرے کم کم
نیند کی اوس نے ان چہروں سے دھو ڈالا تھا
دیس کا درد، فراقِ رخِ محبوب کا غم

دورِ نوبت ہوئی، پھرنے لگے بیزار قدم
زرد فاقوں کے ستائے ہوئے پہرے والے
اہلِ زنداں کے غضب ناک، خروشاں نالے
جن کی باہوں میں پھر اکرتے ہیں بانہیں ڈالے

A Prison Daybreak

Night wasn't over
when the moon stood beside my bed
and said, "You've drunk your sleep to the dregs,
your share of that wine is finished for this night."

My eyes tore themselves from a dream of passion—
they said farewell to my lover's image, still
lingering in the night's stagnant waters
that were spread, like a sheet, over the earth.
Silver whirlpools began their dervish dance
as lotuses of stars fell from the moon's hands.
Some sank. Some rose to the surface,
floated, and opened their petals.
Night and daybreak had fallen desperately
into each other's arms.

In the courtyard,
the prisoners emerged slowly
from a backdrop of gloom. They were shining,
for the dew of sleep had washed, for that moment,
all grief for their country from their eyes,
all agony of separation from their lovers.

But there's a drum, far off. A siren wails.
The famished guards, their faces pale,
begin their reluctant rounds, in step
with stifled screams from torture rooms.
The cries of those who'll be broken on the rack awake.

لذّتِ خواب سے مخمور ہوائیں جاگیں

جیل کی زہر بھری چور صدائیں جاگیں

دور دروازہ کھلا کوئی ، کوئی بند ہوا

دور مچلی کوئی زنجیر، مچل کے روئی

دور اُترا کسی تالے کے جگر میں خنجر

سر پٹکنے لگا رہ رہ کے دریچہ کوئی

گویا پھر خواب سے بیدار ہوئے دشمنِ جاں

سنگ و فولاد سے ڈھالے ہوئے جنّاتِ گراں

جن کے چنگل میں شب و روز ہیں فریاد کناں

میرے بیکار شب و روز کی نازک پریاں

اپنے شہپور کی رہ دیکھ رہی ہیں یہ اسیر

جس کے ترکش میں ہیں اُمّید کے جلتے ہوئے تیر

ناتمام

just as light breezes intoxicated with sleep awake.
Poison awakes. Nothing in the world is asleep.
A door opens in the distance, another is shut.
A chain rasps, then shrieks.
A knife opens a lock's heart, far off,
and a window begins to break its head,
like a madman, against the wind.

So it is the enemies of life awake
and crush the delicate spirit
that keeps me company in my barren despair
while the prisoners and I wait, all day and night,
for a rebel prince of legends to come
with burning arrows, ready to pierce
these tyrant hearts of stone and steel.

سب قتل ہو کے تیرے مقابل سے آئے ہیں

ہم لوگ سرخرو ہیں کہ منزل سے آئے ہیں

شمعِ نظر، خیال کے انجم، جگر کے داغ

جتنے چراغ ہیں، تری محفل سے آئے ہیں

اُٹھ کر تو آ گئے ہیں تری بزم سے مگر

کچھ دل ہی جانتا ہے کہ کس دل سے آئے ہیں

Ghazal

We all were killed
this our final
triumph

    for we did reach the destination
    we met your challenge
    Beloved Revolution

    and returned after dying
    Oh victory

Whether eyes aflame
or minds lit up by suns
or a solitary heart in ashes

    Love
    each final fire
    emerged from your door

    shaped thus
    by your grace or disdain

As such I came away from the evening
everyone still there with you
among the lights

    only the heart felt
    its terrible defeat

    only it knew its desolation

    and it could speak
    only to itself

ہر اک قدم اجل تھا، ہر اک گام زندگی

ہم گھوم پھر کے کوچۂ قاتل سے آئے ہیں

بادِ خزاں کا شکر کرو فیضؔ، جس کے ہاتھ

نامے کسی بہار شمائل سے آئے ہیں

Each footstep meant death
and even the promise of life

    for I've returned from the lane
    where the executioner lives

    I've loitered there
    as if to get some air

    casually
    I've strolled by his door

Faiz
be grateful to autumn

    to its cold winds
    that are seasoned postmen
    carrying letters as mere habit

    from spring

    its custom to announce thus
    that it will surely come

اے حبیبِ عنبر دست!

ایک اجنبی خاتون کے نام
خوشبو کا تحفہ وصول ہونے پر

کسی کے دستِ عنایت نے کنجِ زنداں میں
کیا ہے آج عجب دل نواز بندوبست
مہک رہی ہے فضا زلفِ یار کی صورت
ہوا ہے گرمیُ خوشبو سے اس طرح سرمست
ابھی ابھی کوئی گزرا ہے گل بدن گویا
کہیں قریب سے، گیسو بدوش، غنچہ بدست

لیے ہے بوئے رفاقت اگر ہوائے چمن
تو لاکھ پہرے بٹھائیں قفس پہ ظلم پرست
ہمیشہ سبز رہے گی وہ شاخِ مہر و وفا
کہ جس کے ساتھ بندھی ہے دلوں کی فتح و شکست

یہ شعرِ حافظِ شیراز، اے صبا کہنا
ملے جو تجھ سے کہیں وہ حبیبِ عنبر دست
"خلل پذیر بود ہر بنا کہ می بینی
بجز بنائے محبت کہ خالی از خلل است"

سنٹرل جیل، حیدرآباد
۲۹،۲۸ اپریل ۵۳ء

Fragrant Hands

(For the anonymous woman who sent me
a bouquet of flowers in prison)

A strange arrangement to comfort the heart—
someone has made that possible
in a corner of the cell
with giving, generous hands,

and the air is now so softened,
I compare it with the Beloved's hair,
the air is so drowned,
I think a body, wearing a jewelry of blossoms,
has just passed this way.

And as the air holds itself together,
a bouquet of compassion,
I can say:

Let thousands of watches be set on cages
by those who worship cruelty,
fidelity will always be in bloom—
this fidelity on which are grafted
the defeats and triumphs of the heart.

. . .

Should you, Oh air, ever come across her,
        my friend of fragrant hands,
recite this from Hafiz of Shiraz to her:
        "Nothing in this world is without terrible barriers—
        Except love, but only when it begins."

شامِ فراق، اب نہ پوچھ، آئی اور آ کے ٹل گئی
دل تھا کہ پھر بہل گیا، جاں تھی کہ پھر سنبھل گئی

بزمِ خیال میں ترے حُسن کی شمع جل گئی
درد کا چاند بجھ گیا، ہجر کی رات ڈھل گئی

جب تجھے یاد کر لیا، صبح مہک مہک اُٹھی
جب ترا غم جگا لیا، رات مچل مچل گئی

دل سے تو ہر معاملہ کر کے چلے تھے صاف ہم
کہنے میں ان کے سامنے بات بدل بدل گئی

آخرِ شب کے ہم سفر فیض نجانے کیا ہوئے
رہ گئی کس جگہ صبا، صبح کدھر نکل گئی

جناح ہسپتال کراچی   جولائی ۵۳ء

Ghazal

Ask no more about separation
somehow I lived through its night
    The heart learned to console itself
    life returned to its routines

In the festival of memory
you again were loveliness
lit up by beauty
    The grief of the moon was extinguished
    we were again together in the night

When I remember you
the morning is essence it is perfume it's musk
    And the night
    when I kindle our sorrow
    is longing caught in itself

The heart as such
had settled its every doubt
when I went to tell her we must part
    But on seeing her
    the lips spoke love's unrehearsed words
    and everything changed everything changed

It was the final night Faiz
what happened to those who'd started out with you?
    When did the morning breeze abandon you
    and where on those last miles
    the dawn?

اے روشنیوں کے شہر

سبزہ سبزہ، سوکھ رہی ہے پھیکی، زرد دوپہر
دیواروں کو چاٹ رہا ہے تنہائی کا زہر
دور افق تک گھٹتی، بڑھتی، اُکھتی، گرتی رہتی ہے
کہر کی صورت بے رونق دردوں کی گدلی لہر
بستا ہے، اس کہر کے پیچھے روشنیوں کا شہر

اے روشنیوں کے شہر
کون کہے کس سَمت ہے تیری روشنیوں کی راہ
ہر جانب بے نور کھڑی ہے ہجر کی شہر پناہ
تھک کر ہر سو بیٹھ رہی ہے شوق کی ماند سپاہ

آج مرا دل فکر میں ہے
اے روشنیوں کے شہر
شب خوں سے منھ پھیر نہ جائے ارمانوں کی رو
خیر ہو تیری لیلاؤں کی، ان سب سے کہہ دو
آج کی شب جب دیے جلائیں، اونچی رکھیں لو

لاہور جیل۔ ۲۸ مارچ
منٹگری جیل۔ ۱۵ اپریل ۱۹۵۴ء

32

City of Lights

On each patch of green, from one shade to the next,
the noon is erasing itself by wiping out all color,
becoming pale, desolation everywhere,
the poison of exile painted on the walls.
In the distance,
there are terrible sorrows, like tides:
they draw back, swell, become full, subside.
They've turned the horizon to mist.
And behind that mist is the city of lights,
my city of many lights.

How will I return to you, my city,
where is the road to your lights? My hopes
are in retreat, exhausted by these unlit, broken walls,
and my heart, their leader, is in terrible doubt.

But let all be well, my city, if under
cover of darkness, in a final attack,
my heart leads its reserves of longings
and storms you tonight. Just tell all your lovers
to turn the wicks of their lamps high
so that I may find you, Oh city,
my city of many lights.

گلوں میں رنگ بھرے بادِ نوبہار چلے

چلے بھی آؤ کہ گلشن کا کاروبار چلے

قفس اُداس ہے یارو صبا سے کچھ تو کہو

کہیں تو بہرِ خدا آج ذکرِ یار چلے

کبھی تو صبحِ ترے کنجِ لب سے ہو آغاز

کبھی تو شب سرِ کاکل سے مشکبار چلے

بڑا ہے دردکا رشتہ، یہ دل غریب سہی

تمہارے نام پہ آئیں گے غمگسار چلے

34

Ghazal

Let the breeze pour colors
    into the waiting blossoms

    unlock the warehouses
    where those colors are stored

    Oh Love now return
    so the promised springtime may finally begin

There is weeping in the prisons
    friends say something
    just speak

    today
    if only for the sake of God
    let her name pass through a cage

From the corner of your lips
    let the dawn begin
    at least for once

    and let it be fragrant
    the night which will descend
    when you open your hair

My heart is poor
    it needs no reminding
    but it holds all the wealth of longing

    on hearing your name
    I'll always return

    once again become the one
    to share your sorrow

جو ہم پہ گزری سو گزری مگر شبِ ہجراں
ہمارے اشک تری عاقبت سنوار چلے

حضورِ یار ہوئی دفترِ جنوں کی طلب
گرہ میں لے کے گریباں کا تار تار چلے

مقام، فیض، کوئی راہ میں جچا ہی نہیں
جو کوئے یار سے نکلے تو سوئے دار چلے

منتگری جیل
۲۹؍ جنوری ۵۴ء

Whatever the pain
    I endured its every moment but

    Oh Night of Sorrow you weren't diminished

    my tears made sure
    you would remain a legend
    even in the afterlife

She goes to the office of desires
    to see who's still listed
    in the ledger of lovers

    we are already there waiting
    our shirts ripped to threads

    in our hands those threads
    (proof that we were faithful)
    tied stubbornly into knots

After farewell Oh Faiz
    nothing could hold you back
    nothing at any stop was worthy of desire

    from her street you walked
    straight to the district of executions

    you climbed the steps to the gallows
    lost yourself in the hangman's arms

ہم جو تاریک راہوں میں مارے گئے

ایتھل اور جولیس روز نبرگ کے
خطوط سے متاثر ہو کر لکھی گئی.

تیرے ہونٹوں کے پھولوں کی چاہت میں ہم
دار کی خشک ٹہنی پہ وارے گئے
تیرے ہاتھوں کی شمعوں کی حسرت میں ہم
نیم تاریک راہوں میں مارے گئے

سولیوں پر ہمارے لبوں سے پرے
تیرے ہونٹوں کی لالی لپکتی رہی
تیری زلفوں کی مستی برستی رہی
تیرے ہاتھوں کی چاندی دمکتی رہی

جب گھلی تیری راہوں میں شامِ ستم
ہم چلے آئے، لائے جہاں تک قدم
لب پہ حرفِ غزل، دل میں قندیلِ غم
اپنا غم تھا گواہی ترے حسن کی
دیکھ قائم رہے اس گواہی پہ ہم
ہم جو تاریک راہوں میں مارے گئے

نارسائی اگر اپنی تقدیر تھی
تیری الفت تو اپنی ہی تدبیر تھی
کس کو شکوہ ہے گر شوق کے سلسلے
ہجر کی قتل گاہوں سے سب جا ملے

قتل گاہوں سے چن کر ہمارے علم
اور نکلیں گے عشاق کے قافلے

We who were Executed

*(After reading the letters of
Julius and Ethel Rosenberg)*

I longed for your lips, dreamed of their roses:
I was hanged from the dry branch of the scaffold.
I wanted to touch your hands, their silver light:
I was murdered in the half-light of dim lanes.

And there where you were crucified,
so far away from my words,
you still were beautiful:
color kept clinging to your lips—
rapture was still vivid in your hair—
light remained silvering in your hands.

When the night of cruelty merged with the roads you had taken,
I came as far as my feet could bring me,
on my lips the phrase of a song,
my heart lit up only by sorrow.
This sorrow was my testimony to your beauty—
Look! I remained a witness till the end,
I who was killed in the darkest lanes.

It's true—that not to reach you was fate—
but who'll deny that to love you
was entirely in my hands?
So why complain if these matters of desire
brought me inevitably to the execution grounds?

جن کی راہِ طلب سے ہمارے قدم

مختصر کر چلے درد کے فاصلے

کر چلے جن کی خاطر جہاں گیر ہم

جاں گنوا کر تری دلبری کا بھرم

ہم جو تاریک راہوں میں مارے گئے

منٹگری جیل

۱۵؍ مئی سنہ ۵۴ء

Why complain? Holding up our sorrows as banners,
new lovers will emerge
from the lanes where we were killed
and embark, in caravans, on those highways of desire.
It's because of them that we shortened the distances of sorrow,
it's because of them that we went out to make the world our own,
we who were murdered in the darkest lanes.

شام

اس طرح ہے کہ ہر اک پیڑ کوئی مندر ہے
کوئی اُجڑا ہوا' بے نور پُرانا مندر
ڈھونڈتا ہے جو خرابی کے بہانے کب سے
چاک ہر بام' ہر اک در کا دم آخر ہے
آسماں کوئی پروہت ہے جو ہر بام تلے
جسم پر راکھ ملے، ماتھے پہ سیندور ملے
سرنگوں بیٹھا ہے چپ چاپ نہ جانے کب سے
اس طرح ہے کہ پس پردہ کوئی ساحر ہے

جس نے آفاق پہ پھیلایا ہے یوں سحر کا دام
دامنِ وقت سے پیوست ہے یوں دامنِ شام
اب کبھی شام بجھے گی نہ اندھیرا ہوگا
اب کبھی رات ڈھلے گی نہ سویرا ہوگا

آسماں آس لیے ہے کہ یہ جادو ٹوٹے
چپ کی زنجیر کٹے، وقت کا دامن چھوٹے
دے کوئی سنکھ دہائی' کوئی پایل بولے
کوئی بت جاگے، کوئی سانولی گھونگھٹ کھولے

Evening

The trees are dark ruins of temples,
seeking excuses to crumble
since who knows when—
their roofs are cracked,
their doors lost to ancient winds.
And the sky is a priest,
saffron marks on his forehead,
ashes smeared on his body.
He sits by the temples, worn to a shadow, not looking up.

Some terrible magician, hidden behind curtains,
has hypnotized Time
so this evening is a net
in which the twilight is caught.
Now darkness will never come—
and there will never be morning.

The sky waits for this spell to be broken,
for History to tear itself from this net,
for Silence to break its chains
so that a symphony of conch shells
may wake up the statues
and a beautiful, dark goddess,
her anklets echoing, may unveil herself.

قیدِ تنہائی

دُور آفاق پہ لہرائی کوئی نُور کی لہر
خواب ہی خواب میں بیدار ہوا دردکا شہر
خواب ہی خواب میں بے تاب نظر ہونے لگی
عدم آبادِ جدائی میں سحر ہونے لگی
کاسۂ دل میں بھر دی اپنی صبوحی میں نے
گھول کر تلخیِ دیروز میں امروز کا زہر

دُور آفاق پہ لہرائی کوئی نُور کی لہر
آنکھ سے دور کسی صبح کی تمہید لیے
کوئی نغمہ، کوئی خوشبو، کوئی کافصورت
بے خبر سے گزری، پریشانیِ اُمید لیے
گھول کر تلخیِ دیروز میں امروز کا زہر
حسرتِ روز ملاقات رقم کی میں نے
دیس پردیس کے یارانِ قدح خوار کے نام
حُسنِ آفاق، جمالِ لب و رخسار کے نام

زندان قلعۂ لاہور
مارچ ۱۹۵۹ء

44

Solitary Confinement

Wave of light on the horizon:
the city of grief awakes
and the eye too is restless—
but truly the city sleeps, the eye too sleeps.

Here in this dark where separation is endless,
I see dawn: I take it through the bars
and pour it into the heart, the cup
where I mix yesterday's poison with today's exile.
I drink.

A little light on the far, far horizon:
it brings news of another dawn, farther out, behind the horizon:
a song, the ghost of musk, the ravishing face of love
pass through here where there is no hope;
they pass and I'm again alone, restless with terrible hope.

I drink the poison and I drink the faint light.
I say, "To life,"
and long for my friends at home
and in countries I'll never see.
With them I used to raise a glass
to this planet
and to the beauty of woman.

ترے غم کو جاں کی تلاش تھی ترے جاں نثار چلے گئے
تری رہ میں کرتے تھے سرِ طلب، سرِ رہگزار چلے گئے

تری کج ادائی سے ہار کے شبِ انتظار چلی گئی
مرے ضبطِ حال سے روٹھ کر مرے غمگسار چلے گئے

نہ سوالِ وصل، نہ عرضِ غم، نہ حکایتیں نہ شکایتیں
ترے عہد میں دلِ زار کے سبھی اختیار چلے گئے

Ghazal

Your sorrow is in search of someone
willing to spill his blood
but they who once lined the roads

    ready to give up this life
    at a moment's notice
    for you

    have left
    no longer to be found

Beloved
the night waited with me for you
at dawn it admitted defeat and left

    my consolers also departed
    hurt to find my eyes
    without tears

    let down that I held back my grief

Nothing's left now
no possibility of the night of love
and no way to show even a glimpse of pain

    there's no room for complaints
    no margins allowed for suggestions

    Tyrant
    it's your era
    the restless heart's lost its every right

یہ ہیں تھے جن کے لباس پر سہرہ سیاہی لکھی گئی

یہی داغ تھے جو سجا کے ہم سرِ بزمِ یار چلے گئے

نہ رہا جنونِ رُخِ وفا، یہ رسن یہ دار کرو گے کیا

جنہیں جُرمِ عشق پہ ناز تھا وہ گناہ گار چلے گئے

جولائی ۵۹ء

It was me
it was my shirt
that was printed

> with blood on the streets
> darkened there with inks of accusation

> I declared these stains a new fashion
> and went to mingle with the guests
> at my lover's home

Nowhere anymore
that abandon of passion

> no one wears fidelity's raw fabrics

> Hangman
> what will you do with that rope?
> who's asked you to build the scaffold?

> those once proud to be accused of love
> they all have vanished

آ گئی فصلِ سکوں چاک گریباں والو
رِسل گئے ہونٹ، کوئی زخم سِلے یا نہ سِلے

دوستو بزم سجاؤ کہ بہار آئی ہے
کھل گئے زخم، کوئی پھول کِھلے یا نہ کِھلے

اپریل ۱۹۷۲ء

50

Poem

You who wear shirts
ripped at the collars:

    it has come:
    the great calm
    with its harvest of silence:

    all lips have been sewn,
    perhaps some wounds also.

And rebels,
my friends:

    fill your vases with water
    for spring is here:

    in this blossoming
    of wounds,

    some roses may also.

ملاقات مری

ساری دیوار سیہ ہوگئی تا حلقۂ بام
رستے بجھ گئے رخصت ہوئے رہگیر تمام
اپنی تنہائی سے گویا ہوئی پھر رات مری
ہو نہ ہو آج پھر آئی ہے ملاقات مری
اک ہتھیلی پہ حنا، ایک ہتھیلی پہ لہو
اک نظر زہر لیے ایک نظر میں دارو
دیر سے منزلِ دل میں کوئی آیا نہ گیا
فرقتِ درد میں بے آب ہوا تختۂ داغ
کس سے کہیے کہ بھرے رنگ سے زخموں کے ایاغ
اور پھر خود ہی چلی آئی ملاقات مری
آشنا موت جو دشمن بھی ہے غمخوار بھی ہے
وہ جو ہم لوگوں کی قاتل بھی ہے دلدار بھی ہے

Two Elegies

1. Appointments

The walls, each inch of them, have turned black.
Darkness has climbed up to the noose of the ceiling.
All roads have been stamped out, their lights gone out.
Everyone has taken leave. I am alone,
and it's night, nothing but night.
It seems desolation will be my only companion,
for whatever may or may not be,
once again she has come to me for the night,
her one hand dyed red like a bride's,
the other wet with the blood of her victims,
her one eye poison, the other wine.

Years have passed since my heart's been anyone's destination,
and its wounds, in this desolation,
have lost their sheen—
Whom can I possibly ask to pour color into them?

But suddenly she is here, come
once again, without my asking,
that familiar one, Beloved death,
my enemy who erases sorrows like a friend,
my murderer who's also my lover.

ختم ہوئی بارشِ سنگ

ناگہاں آج مرے تارِ نظر سے کٹ کر

ٹکڑے ٹکڑے ہوئے آفاق پہ خورشید و قمر

اب کسی سَمت اندھیرا نہ اُجالا ہوگا

بجھ گئی دل کی طرح راہِ وفا میرے بعد

دوستو! قافلۂ درد کا اب کیا ہوگا

اب کوئی اور کرے پرورشِ گلشنِ غم

دوستو ختم ہوئی دیدۂ تر کی شبنم

تھم گیا شورِ جنوں ختم ہوئی بارشِ سنگ

خاک رہ آج لیے ہے لبِ دلدار کا رنگ

کوئے جاناں میں کھلا میرے لہو کا پرچم

دیکھیے دیتے ہیں کس کس کو صدا میرے بعد

"کون ہوتا ہے حریفِ مے مردافگنِ عشق

ہے مکرّر لبِ ساقی پہ صلا میرے بعد"

نومبر ۱۹۷۶ء

2. The Rain of Stones is Finished

*(For Hassan Nasir, tortured to death
in the Lahore Fort, 1959)*

Today as I stared, suddenly a string snapped,
and the moon and sun were smashed in the sky.
No darkness is left in any corner, and no light—
behind me the road of fidelity lies broken,
    its lights extinguished, like my heart;
and nothing remains ahead. Friends, what will happen now?

Convoys of pain bearing cargoes of love must keep moving,
but someone else must now wave them forward.
And others must tend the garden where ardor blooms—
I can't: the dew of my eyes has dried: I won't weep again.
All rapture, the pure madness of passion, has ceased,
    and no one's left to bear the rain of stones.

That road behind me: it was always the Beloved's street.
It is now the color of her lips;
my blood, like a flag, has been unfurled there.
I have nothing left to give.

And a glass is being filled again.
Friends, let one of you now come forward,
for the cry has begun: "Who'll dare to drink this wine of love
    that is blood and poison? Who?"
This is the cry in the tavern after I'm gone.

رنگ ہے دل کا مرے

تم نہ آئے تھے تو ہر چیز وہی تھی کہ جو ہے
آسماں حدِ نظر، راہگزر راہگزر، شیشہ مے شیشہ مے
اور اب شیشہ مے، راہگزر، رنگِ فلک
رنگ ہے دل کا مرے، "خونِ جگر ہونے تک"
چمپئی رنگ کبھی راحتِ دیدار کا رنگ
سرمئی رنگ کہ ہے ساعتِ بیزار کا رنگ
زرد پتوں کا، خس و خار کا رنگ
سرخ پھولوں کا دہکتے ہوئے گلزار کا رنگ

زہر کا رنگ، لہو رنگ، شبِ تار کا رنگ
آسماں، راہگزر، شیشہ مے،
کوئی بھیگا ہوا دامن، کوئی دُکھتی ہوئی رگ
کوئی ہر لحظہ بدلتا ہوا آئینہ ہے

اب جو آئے ہو تو ٹھہرو کہ کوئی رنگ، کوئی رُت، کوئی شے
ایک جگہ پر ٹھہرے،
پھر سے اک بار ہر اک چیز وہی ہو کہ جو ہے
آسماں حدِ نظر، راہگزر راہگزر، شیشہ مے شیشہ مے

ماسکو
اگست ۱۹۶۳ء

56

Before You Came

Before you came,
things were as they should be:
the sky was the dead-end of sight,
the road was just a road, wine merely wine.

Now everything is like my heart,
a color at the edge of blood:
the grey of your absence, the color of poison, of thorns,
the gold when we meet, the season ablaze,
the yellow of autumn, the red of flowers, of flames,
and the black when you cover the earth
with the coal of dead fires.

And the sky, the road, the glass of wine?
The sky is a shirt wet with tears,
the road a vein about to break,
and the glass of wine a mirror in which
the sky, the road, the world keep changing.

Don't leave now that you're here—
Stay. So the world may become like itself again:
so the sky may be the sky,
the road a road,
and the glass of wine not a mirror, just a glass of wine.

پاس رہو

تم مرے پاس رہو
میرے قاتل، مرے دلدار، مرے پاس رہو
جس گھڑی رات چلے،
آسمانوں کا لہو پی کے سیہ رات چلے
مرہم مشک لیے، نشترِ الماس لیے
بین کرتی ہوئی، ہنستی ہوئی، گاتی نکلے
درد کے کاسنی پازیب بجاتی نکلے
جس گھڑی سینوں میں ڈوبے ہوئے دل
آستینوں میں نہاں ہاتھوں کی رہ تکنے لگیں
آس لیے
اور بچوں کے بلکنے کی طرح قلقلِ مے
بہرِ ناسودگی چلے تو منائے نہ بنے
جب کوئی بات بنائے نہ بنے
جب نہ کوئی بات چلے
جس گھڑی رات چلے
جس گھڑی ماتمی، سنسان، سیہ رات چلے
پاس رہو
میرے قاتل، مرے دلدار مرے پاس رہو!

ماسکو
1963ء

58

Be Near Me

You who demolish me, you whom I love,
be near me. Remain near me when evening,
drunk on the blood of the skies,
becomes night, in its one hand
a perfumed balm, in the other
a sword sheathed in the diamond of stars.

Be near me when night laments or sings,
or when it begins to dance,
its steel-blue anklets ringing with grief.

Be here when longings, long submerged
in the heart's waters, resurface
and everyone begins to look:
Where is the assassin? In whose sleeve
is hidden the redeeming knife?

And when wine, as it is poured, is the sobbing
of children whom nothing will console—
when nothing holds,
when nothing is:
at that dark hour when night mourns,
be near me, my destroyer, my lover,
be near me.

منظر

رہگزر، سائے، شجر، منزلِ دور، حلقۂ بام
بام پر سینۂ مہتاب کھلا، آہستہ
جس طرح کھولے کوئی بندِ قبا، آہستہ
حلقۂ بام تلے، سایوں کا ٹھہرا ہوا نیل
نیل کی جھیل
جھیل میں چپکے سے تیرا، کسی پتے کا حباب
ایک پل تیرا، چلا، پھوٹ گیا، آہستہ

بہت آہستہ، بہت ہلکا، خنک رنگِ شراب
میرے شیشے میں ڈھلا، آہستہ
شیشہ و جام، صراحی، ترے ہاتھوں کے گلاب
جس طرح دور کسی خواب کا نقش
آپ ہی آپ بنا اور مٹا آہستہ

دل نے دہرایا کوئی حرفِ وفا، آہستہ
تم نے کہا، "آہستہ"
چاند نے جھک کے کہا
"اور ذرا آہستہ"

ماسکو
۱۹۶۳ء

60

Vista

Deserted street, shadows of trees and houses, locked doors—
We watched the moon become a woman,
baring her breast, softly, on the edge of a rooftop.
Below the earth was blue, a lake of stilled shadows,
on which a leaf, the bubble of a second, floated
and then burst, softly.
Pale, very pale, gently, very slowly,
wine that is cold color
was poured into my glass,
and the roses of your hands, the decanter and the glass,
were, like the outline
of a dream, in focus, for a moment.
Then they melted, softly.
My heart once again promised love, softly.
You said, "But softly."
The moon, breathing as it went down, said,
"More, yet more softly."

لہو کا سُراغ

کہیں نہیں ہے کہیں بھی نہیں لہو کا سراغ
نہ دستِ و ناخنِ قاتل نہ آستیں پہ نشاں
نہ سرخئ لبِ خنجر نہ رنگِ نوکِ سناں
نہ خاک پر کوئی دھبّا نہ بام پر کوئی داغ
کہیں نہیں ہے کہیں بھی نہیں لہو کا سراغ
نہ صرفِ خدمتِ شاہاں کہ خوںبہا دیتے
نہ دیں کی نذر کہ بیعانہ جزا دیتے
نہ رزم گاہ میں برسا کہ معتبر ہوتا
کسی علَم پہ رقم ہو کے مشتہر ہوتا
پکارتا رہا، بے آسرا، یتیم لہو
کسی کو بہرِ ساعت نہ وقت تھا نہ دماغ
نہ مدّعی، نہ شہادت، حساب پاک ہوا
یہ خونِ خاک نشیناں تھا، رزقِ خاک ہوا

کراچی
جنوری ۱۹۶۵ء

62

In Search of Vanished Blood

There's no sign of blood, not anywhere.
I've searched everywhere.
The executioner's hands are clean, his nails transparent.
The sleeves of each assassin are spotless.
No sign of blood: no trace of red,
not on the edge of the knife, none on the point of the sword.
The ground is without stains, the ceiling white.

This blood which has disappeared without leaving a trace
isn't part of written history: who will guide me to it?
It wasn't spilled in service of emperors—
    it earned no honor, had no wish granted.
It wasn't offered in rituals of sacrifice—
    no cup of absolution holds it in a temple.
It wasn't shed in any battle—
    no one calligraphed it on banners of victory.

But, unheard, it still kept crying out to be heard.
No one had the time to listen, no one the desire.
It kept crying out, this orphan blood,
but there was no witness. No case was filed.
From the beginning this blood was nourished only by dust.
Then it turned to ashes, left no trace, became food for dust.

63

یہاں سے شہر کو دیکھو

یہاں سے شہر کو دیکھو تو حلقہ در حلقہ
کھنچی ہے جیل کی صورت ہر ایک سمت فصیل
ہر ایک راہ گزر گردشِ اسیراں ہے
نہ سنگِ میل، نہ منزل، نہ مخلصی کی سبیل

جو کوئی تیز چلے رہ تو پوچھتا ہے خیال
کہ ٹوکنے کوئی للکار کیوں نہیں آئی
جو کوئی ہاتھ ہلائے تو وہم کو ہے سوال
کوئی چھنک، کوئی جھنکار کیوں نہیں آئی؟

یہاں سے شہر کو دیکھو تو ساری خلقت میں
نہ کوئی صاحبِ تمکیں، نہ کوئی والیِ ہوش
ہر ایک مردِ جواں مجسّرم رسن بہ گلو
ہر اک حسینۂ رعنا، کنیز حلقہ بگوش

جو سائے دور چراغوں کے گرد لرزاں ہیں
نہ جانے محفلِ غم ہے کہ بزمِ جام و سبو
جو رنگ ہر درد دیوار پر پریشاں ہیں
یہاں سے کچھ نہیں کھلتا یہ پھول ہیں کہ لہو

کراچی۔ مارچ ۱۹۶۵ء

64

The City from Here

When you look at the city from here,
this is its pattern: circles within circles,
each outer one a wall imprisoning the inner,
no escape in any direction. Each road,
each street seems viciously trapped, a prisoner
with no milestone, no destination,
and no occasion for fidelity.

When someone quickens his step, you think
at any moment he'll be ordered to halt.
When someone raises his arm, you wait
to hear the sudden chains of a handcuff.

When you look at the city from here,
among the populace you see no one
with any dignity or pride. No one is aware.
Each young man walks like a criminal,
as if the scaffold's shadow were on his neck.
Every beautiful woman's bracelets mark her a slave.

There are flames dancing in the farthest corners,
throwing their shadows on a group of mourners.
Or are they lighting up a feast of poetry and wine?
From here you cannot tell, as you cannot tell
whether the color clinging to those distant doors and walls
is that of roses or of blood.

بلیک آوٹ

جب سے بے نور ہوئی ہیں شمعیں

خاک میں ڈھونڈتا پھرتا ہوں نہ جانے کس جا

کھو گئی ہیں میری دونوں آنکھیں

تم جو واقف ہو بتاؤ کوئی پہچان مری

اس طرح ہے کہ ہر اک رگ میں اتر آیا ہے

موج در موج کسی زہر کا قاتل دریا

تیرا ارمان، تری یاد لیے جان مری

جانے کس موج میں غلطاں ہے کہاں دل میرا

ایک پل ٹھہرو کہ اس پار کسی دنیا سے

برق آئے مری جانب، ید بیضا لے کر

اور مری آنکھوں کے گم گشتہ گہر

جامِ ظلمت سے سیہ مست

نئی آنکھوں کے شب تاب گہر

لوٹا مادے

ایک پل ٹھہرو کہ دریا کا کہیں پاٹ لگے

اور نیا دل میرا

زہر میں ڈھل کے، فنا ہو کے

کسی گھاٹ لگے

پھر پیئوں نذرِ نئے دیدہ و دل لے کے چلوں

حسن کی مدح کروں، شوق کا مضمون لکھوں

ستمبر ۱۹۷۵ء

Black Out

(Written during the India-Pakistan war of 1965)

Ever since the lights failed,
I have been searching to see how I could see.
Where have my eyes strayed in the dust?

You who know, give me proof.
Describe me to myself.

A bitter river rages in my veins.
And my heart, still longing for you,
flows on its poisonous waves.

Wait a little: perhaps from some other world
the hand of a prophet, carved in lightning,
is bringing me pearls for my lost eyes.

Wait till the river is stilled
and my submerged heart, annulled like a Sufi's,
is washed up, cleansed, on a welcoming shore.

I will then begin a new translation of hope.
I will complete the texts of love.

سوچنے دو

(آندرے وزینیسنسکی کے نام)

اک ذرا سوچنے دو

اس خیاباں میں

جو اس لحظہ بیاباں بھی نہیں

کون سی شاخ میں بھول آئے تھے سب سے پہلے

کون بے رنگ ہوئی رنج و تعب سے پہلے

اور اب سے پہلے

کس گھڑی کس کون سے موسم میں یہاں

خون کا قحط پڑا

گل کی شہ رگ پہ کڑا

وقت پڑا

سوچنے دو

اک ذرا سوچنے دو

یہ بھرا شہر جو اب وادیُ ویراں بھی نہیں

اس میں کس وقت کہاں

آگ لگی تھی پہلے

اس کے صف بستہ دریچوں میں سے کس میں اوّل

زہ ہوئی سرخ شعاعوں کی کمان

کس جگہ جوت جگی تھی پہلے

سوچنے دو

Let Me Think

(For Andrei Voznesensky)

Let me think
just for a while . . .
In that withered garden,
more bare than even a desert now,
which branch first burst into blossom?
And which was the first to lose its colors
before everything succumbed to regret?
At what exact moment
were the trees drained of blood
so when the veins snapped,
nothing could be saved?
Oh, let me think . . .

Yes, let me think for a while . . .
Where in that once-teeming city,
forsaken even by loneliness now,
was that fire first lit
that burned it down to ruins?
From which of its blacked-out rows of windows
flew the first arrows, tipped with blood?
In which home was the first candle lit?
Let me think . . .

ہم سے اُس دیس کا تم نام و نشاں پوچھتے ہو

جس کی تاریخ نہ جغرافیہ اب یاد آئے

اور یاد آئے تو محبوبِ گزشتہ کی طرح

روبرو آنے سے جی گھبرائے

ہاں مگر جیسے کوئی

ایسے محبوب یا محبوبہ کا دل رکھنے کو

آنکلتا ہے کبھی رات، بتانے کے لیے

ہم اب اُس عمر کو آ پہنچے ہیں جب ہم بھی یونہی

دل سے مل آتے ہیں بس رسم نبھانے کے لیے

دل کی کیا پوچھتے ہو

سوچنے دو

ماسکو

مارچ مہینہ ۱۹۷۶ء

You ask me about that country
whose details now escape me.
I don't remember its geography,
nothing of its history.
And should I visit it in memory,
it would be as I would a past lover,
after years, for a night,
no longer restless with passion, with no fear of regret.
I have reached that age
when one visits the heart merely as a courtesy,
the way one keeps in touch
with any old neighbor.
So don't question me about the heart.
Just let me think.

ہارٹ اٹیک

درد اتنا تھا کہ اس رات دلِ وحشی نے
ہر رگِ جاں سے اُلجھنا چاہا
ہر بنِ مو سے ٹپکنا چاہا
اور کہیں دور ترے صحن میں گویا
پتا پتا مرے افسردہ لہو میں ڈھل کر
حسنِ مہتاب سے آزردہ نظر آنے لگا
میرے ویرانۂ تن میں گویا
سارے دُکھتے ہوئے ریشوں کی طنابیں کھل کر
سلسلہ وار پتا دینے لگیں
رخصتِ قافلۂ شوق کی تیاری کا
اور جب یاد کی بجھتی ہوئی شمعوں میں نظر آیا کہیں
ایک پل آخری لمحہ تری دلداری کا
درد اتنا تھا کہ اس سے بھی گزرنا چاہا
ہم نے چاہا بھی، مگر دل نہ ٹھہرنا چاہا

۱۹۷۶ء

The Heart Gives Up

Such was its pain that night:
the heart wanted to grip the veins
till the pores would open and its blood rush out.
It was as if somewhere far off,
as if in your courtyard,
each leaf, rinsed in my aching blood,
had wearied of the moon's lustre,
such beauty no longer sufferable.
Such was the heart's pain:
that the body seemed a desert
and the veins, those torn ropes, loosened,
were giving notice that life's caravan,
its cargo emptying, was about to depart.
And when memory, for a moment, was a brief candle,
lighting up the consolation that you are,
it wasn't enough.
Something told me, "Linger, don't leave,"
but the heart didn't waver, it didn't wish to stay.

حذر کرو مرے تن سے

بسے تو کیسے بسے قتلِ عام کا میلہ
کسے بھائے گا میرے لہو کا واویلا
مرے نزار بدن میں لہو ہی کتنا ہے
چراغ ہو کوئی روشن نہ کوئی جام بھرے
نہ اس سے آگ ہی بھڑکے نہ اسے پیاس بجھے
مرے فگار بدن میں لہو ہی کتنا ہے
مگر وہ زہرِ ہلاہل بھرا ہے نس نس میں
جسے بھی چھیدو ہر اک بوند قہر افعی ہے
ہر اک کشید ہے صدیوں کے دردِ حسرت کی
ہر اک میں مہرِ بلب غیظ و غم کی گرمی ہے

حذر کرو مرے تن سے یہ سَم کا دریا ہے
حذر کرو کہ مرا تن وہ چوبِ صحرا ہے
جسے جلاؤ تو صحنِ چمن میں دیکھیں گے

بجائے سرو و سمن میری ہڈیوں کے بول
اسے بکھیرا تو دشت و دمن میں بکھرے گی
بجائے مشکِ صبا، میری جانِ نار کی دھول
حذر کرو کہ مرا دل لہو کا پیاسا ہے   مارچ ۱۹۷۴ء

74

Stay Away from Me (Bangladesh I)

How can I embellish this carnival of slaughter,
  how decorate the massacre?
Whose attention could my lamenting blood attract?
There's almost no blood in my rawboned body
and what's left
isn't enough to burn as oil in the lamp,
not enough to fill a wineglass.
It can feed no fire,
extinguish no thirst.
There's a poverty of blood in my ravaged body—
a terrible poison now runs in it.
If you pierce my veins, each drop will foam
  as venom at the cobra's fangs.
Each drop is the anguished longing of ages,
the burning seal of a rage hushed up for years.
Beware of me. My body is a river of poison.
Stay away from me. My body is a parched log in the desert.
If you burn it, you won't see the cypress or the jasmine,
but my bones blossoming like thorns on the cactus.
If you throw it in the forests,
instead of morning perfumes, you'll scatter
the dust of my seared soul.
So stay away from me. Because I'm thirsting for blood.

تہ بہ تہ دل کی کدورت

میری آنکھوں میں اُمنڈ آئی تو کچھ چارہ نہ تھا

چارہ گر کی مان لی

اور میں نے گرد آلود آنکھوں کو لہو سے دھو لیا

میں نے گرد آلود آنکھوں کو لہو سے دھو لیا

اور اب ہر شکل و صورت

عالمِ موجود کی ہر ایک شے

ہر شجر مینارِ خوں، ہر پھول خونیں دیدہ ہے

میری آنکھوں کے لہو سے اس طرح ہم رنگ ہے

ہر نظر اک تارِ خوں، ہر عکس خوں مالیدہ ہے

خورشید کا کندن لہو

موجِ خوں جب تک رواں رہتی ہے اس کا سُرخ رنگ

مہتاب کی چاندی لہو

جذبۂ شوق شہادت، درد، غیظ و غم کا رنگ

ہنسنوں کا ہنسنا بھی لہو

اور تھم جائے تو کالا کر

راتوں کا رونا بھی لہو

فقط نفرت کا، شب کا، موت کا

ہر اک رنگ کے ماتم کا رنگ

چارہ گر ایسا نہ ہونے دے

کہیں سے لا کوئی سیلابِ اشک

آبِ وضو

جس میں دُھل جائیں تو شاید دُھل سکے

میری آنکھوں، میری گرد آلود آنکھوں کا لہو

۳۰ اپریل ۱۹۷۱ء

76

Bangladesh II

This is how my sorrow became visible:
its dust, piling up for years in my heart,
finally reached my eyes,

the bitterness now so clear that
I had to listen when my friends
told me to wash my eyes with blood.

Everything at once was tangled in blood—
each face, each idol, red everywhere.
Blood swept over the sun, washing away its gold.

The moon erupted with blood, its silver extinguished.
The sky promised a morning of blood,
and the night wept only blood.

The trees hardened into crimson pillars.
All flowers filled their eyes with blood.
And every glance was an arrow,

each pierced image blood. This blood
—a river crying out for martyrs—
flows on in longing. And in sorrow, in rage, in love.

Let it flow. Should it be dammed up,
there will only be hatred cloaked in colors of death.
Don't let this happen, my friends,

bring all my tears back instead,
a flood to purify my dust-filled eyes,
to wash this blood forever from my eyes.

آرزو

مجھے معجزوں پہ یقیں نہیں مگر آرزو ہے کہ جب قضا

مجھے بزمِ دہر سے لے چلے

تو پھر ایک بار یہ اذن دے

کہ لحد سے لوٹ کے آ سکوں

ترے در پہ آ کے صدا کروں

تجھے غمگسار کی ہو طلب تو ترے حضور میں آ رہوں

یہ نہ ہو تو سوئے رہِ عدم میں پھر ایک بار روانہ ہوں

Desire

I have certainly
no faith in miracles, yet I long
that when death comes to take me
from this great song
of a world, it permits me to return
to your door and knock
and knock
and call out: "If you need someone

to share your anguish, your simplest pain,
then let me be the one.
If not, let me again

embark, this time never
to return, in that final direction,
forever."

اٹَک آباد کی شام

جب سورج نے جاتے جاتے
اٹَک آباد کے نیلے افق سے
اپنے سنہری جام
میں ڈھالی
سرخیِ اوّلِ شام

اور یہ جام
تمھارے سامنے رکھ کر
تم سے کیا کلام

کہا پر نام
اُٹھو
اور اپنے تن کی سیج سے اُٹھ کر

ایک شیریں پیغام
ثبت کر دو اس شام
کسی کے نام

کنارِ جام
شاید تم یہ مان گئیں اور تم نے
اپنے لبِ گلفام

کیے انعام
کسی کے نام

کنارِ جام
یا شاید
تم اپنے تن کی سیج پہ سیج کر

80

Evening in Ashkabaad*

When the sun,
just as it was leaving,
poured—from the tilted
horizon of this city—
the blazing reds that announce evening
into a cup of gold
and then, placing that cup beside your bed,
spoke thus,

> "Greetings.
> Wake up.
> Raise yourself from this bed
> your body so sensuously haunts
> and stamp the rim of this cup
> with the seal of your lips,
> a sweet, sweet message
> to someone, to anyone,"

perhaps you agreed
and did just that,
gifting the roses of your lips
on the edge of the cup,
or perhaps you heard absolutely nothing,
so deep you were in slumber,

* *Capital of Turkmen Republic in the Soviet Union.*

81

تھیں یوں محوِ آرام
کہ رستہ تکتے تکتے
بجھ گئی شمعِ جام
اشک آباد کے نیلے اُفق پر
غارت ہوگئی شام

۱۹۴۲ء

so oblivious, so intoxicated with dreams,
that the one candle someone had lit
to light the road you would have taken,
gave up, extinguished itself
after gazing and gazing
at the street
for any sign of you,
and on the blue horizon of this city
the evening burned itself completely to ash.

پاؤں سے لہو کو دھو ڈالو

ہم کیا کرتے کس رہ چلتے

ہر راہ میں کانٹے بکھرے تھے

اُن رشتوں کے جو جھوٹ گئے

اُن صدیوں کے یارانوں کے

جو اِک اِک کر کے ٹوٹ گئے

جس راہ چلے، جس سمت گئے

یوں پاؤں لہو لہان ہوئے

سب دیکھنے والے کہتے تھے

یہ کیسی ریت رچائی ہے

یہ مہندی کیوں لگائی ہے

وہ کہتے تھے، کیوں خط و پا

کا ناحق چرچا کرتے ہو

پاؤں سے لہو کو دھو ڈالو!

یہ راہیں جب اُٹ جائیں گی

صورتیں اِن سے پھوٹیں گی

تم دل کو سنبھالو جس میں ابھی

سو طرح کے نشتر ٹوٹیں گے   ۱۹۷۳ء

84

Wash the Blood off Your Feet

What could I have done, gone where?
My feet were bare
and every road was covered with thorns—
of ruined friendships, of loves left behind,
of eras of loyalty that finished, one by one.

Wherever I went, in whatever direction,
my feet were soaked—
there was so much blood
that bystanders couldn't help asking:
What fashion is this, what new tradition?
For what unknown festival have you dyed your feet?

I said nothing, but they went on asking:
Why do you still complain
of the utter famine of love? You're doing it for nothing.
There's no chance for fidelity now.

So wash this blood off your feet, they said.
Let your feet heal.
These roads, now soft with blood, will harden again.
And a hundred new paths will break through their dried mud.
Keep your feet ready for those roads, they said.

And be careful, they said, take care of the heart.
It still has to break
open into a thousand different wounds.
It still has to know knife after knife after knife

ڈھاکہ سے واپسی پر

ہم کہ ٹھہرے اجنبی اتنی مداراتوں کے بعد
پھر بنیں گے آشنا کتنی ملاقاتوں کے بعد

کب نظر میں آئے گی بے داغ سبزے کی بہار
خون کے دھبے دھلیں گے کتنی برساتوں کے بعد

تھے بہت بے درد لمحے ختم دردِ عشق کے
تھیں بہت بے مہر صبحیں مہرباں راتوں کے بعد

دل تو چاہا پر شکستِ دل نے مہلت ہی نہ دی
کچھ گلے شکوے بھی کر لیتے مناجاتوں کے بعد

اُن سے جو کہنے گئے تھے فیض جاں صدقہ کیے
اَن کہی ہی رہ گئی وہ بات سب باتوں کے بعد

۱۹۷۴ء

On My Return from Dhaka (Bangladesh III)*

After those many encounters, that easy intimacy,
        we are strangers now—
After how many meetings will we be that close again?

When will we again see a spring of unstained green?
After how many monsoons will the blood be washed
        from the branches?

So relentless was the end of love, so heartless—
After the nights of tenderness, the dawns were pitiless,
        so pitiless.

And so crushed was the heart that though it wished,
        it found no chance
—after the entreaties, after the despair—for us to
        quarrel once again as old friends.

Faiz, what you'd gone to say, ready to offer everything,
        even your life—
those healing words remained unspoken after all else had
        been said.

* Revisited after the massacre.

بہار آئی

بہار آئی تو جیسے یکبار
لوٹ آئے ہیں پھر عدم سے
وہ خواب سارے، شباب سارے
جو تیرے ہونٹوں پہ مر مٹے تھے
جو مٹ کے ہر بار پھر جیے تھے
نکھر گئے ہیں گلاب سارے
جو تیری یادوں سے مشکبو ہیں
جو تیرے عشاق کا لہو
ابل پڑے ہیں عذاب سارے
ملالِ احوالِ دوستاں بھی
خمارِ آغوشِ مہ وشاں بھی
غبارِ خاطر کے باب سارے
ترے ہمارے
سوال سارے جواب سارے
بہار آئی تو کھل گئے ہیں
نئے سرے سے حساب سارے

اپریل ۱۹۶۵ء

It is Spring Again

It is spring. And the ledger is opened again.
From the abyss where they were frozen,
those days suddenly return, those days
that passed away from your lips, that died
with all our kisses, unaccounted.
The roses return: they are your fragrance;
they are the blood of your lovers.
Sorrow returns. I go through my pain
and the agony of friends still lost in the memory
of moon-silver arms, the caresses of vanished women.
I go through page after page. There are no answers,
and spring has come once again asking
the same questions, reopening account after account.

ناظم حکمت

زنداں سے ایک خط

مری جان تجھ کو بتلاؤں، بہت نازک یہ نکتہ ہے
بدل جاتا ہے انساں جب مکاں اس کا بدلتا ہے!
مجھے زنداں میں پیار آنے لگا ہے اپنے خوابوں پر
جو شب کو نیند اپنے مہرباں ہاتھوں سے
وا کرتی ہے در اس کا
تو اگرتی ہے ہر دیوار اس کی میرے قدموں پر
یں ایسے غرق ہو جاتا ہوں اس دم اپنے خوابوں میں
کہ جیسے اک کرن ٹھہرے ہوئے پانی پہ گرتی ہے
یں ان لمحوں میں کتنا سرخوش و دلشاد پھرتا ہوں
جہاں کی جگمگاتی وسعتوں میں کس قدر آزاد پھرتا ہوں
جہاں درد و الم کا نام ہے کوئی نہ زنداں ہے
"تو پھر بیدار ہونا کس قدر تم پر گراں ہوگا؟"
نہیں ایسا نہیں ہے۔ میری جان! میرا یہ قصہ ہے
یں اپنے غم و ہمت سے
وہی کچھ بخشتا ہوں نیند کو جو اس کا حصہ ہے

A Letter from Prison

My love, let me share
this most delicate matter with you:
a man is altered by a new home.

Here I've begun to fall in love with my dreams:
for at night when sleep,
with her warm, compassionate hands, opens the gate,
the prison walls collapse at my feet.
At that moment I'm drowned in my dreams
the way a ray falls into still waters.
I walk out and roam free,
filled with relentless joy—
how freely I roam
in wide, lit up spaces
where no word is found for sorrow and pain,
no word for prison.

"Then how crushing it will be
for you to wake up?"

No, that isn't so—my love!
Let me tell you one more thing:
with sheer strength, with stubborn will,
I bestow only those dreams on my sleep
that it has already claimed,
the ones that are its necessary share.

*Translated from Faiz's Urdu version of a poem by
the Turkish poet Nazim Hikmet)*

91

ویرا کے نام

اُس نے کہا آؤ،

اُس نے کہا ٹھہرو

مسکاؤ کہا اس نے

مر جاؤ کہا اس نے

میں آیا،

میں ٹھہر گیا،

مسکایا

اور مر بھی گیا

یہ: ناظم حکمت کی روسی بیوی

For Vera

She said Come
She said Stay
Smile she said
She said Die

I came
I didn't leave
Yes, I smiled
And I even died

*(Translated from Faiz's Urdu version of a poem by
Nazim Hikmet addressed to his Russian wife, Vera)*

اولگٹر عمر علی سلیمان

صحرا کی رات

کہیں بھی شبنم کہیں نہیں ہے
عجب، کہ شبنم کہیں نہیں ہے
نہ سردِ خورشید کی جبیں پر
کسی کے رُخ پر، نہ آستیں پر
ذرا سی شبنم کہیں نہیں ہے
پسے ہوئے پتھروں کی موجیں
خموش و ساکن
حرارتِ ماہِ نیم شب میں سلگ رہی ہیں
اور شبنم کہیں نہیں ہے
برہنہ پاغول گیدڑوں کے
لگار ہے ہیں بنوں میں بھٹے
کہ آج شبنم کہیں نہیں ہے
ببول کے استخواں کے ڈھانچے
پکارتے ہیں
نہیں ہے شبنم، کہیں نہیں ہے

٭: تاجکستان کا ممتاز نوجوان شاعر

A Night in the Desert

There's no dew
anywhere, so
strange that there's no dew
anywhere, not
on the forehead

of the cold sun,
not on anyone's cheek,
not on any sleeve.
Nowhere is there
even a trace of dew.

Crushed rocks, crushed stones:
they are silent, calm.
But their waves are beginning to burn
under the midnight moon.
And there's no dew anywhere.

The naked feet
of herds of jackals
are beating down the floors of jungles,
theirs the only celebration
that there's no dew anywhere.

And skeletons of stripped desert bushes
are also calling out
with a rattle of their bones
that there's no dew,
no dew anywhere.

سفید، دُھند لائی روشنی میں
ہیں دشت کی چھاتیاں برہنہ
ترس رہی ہیں جو حسنِ انساں لیے کہ شبنم کا ایک قطرہ
کہیں پہ برسے
یہ چاند بھی سرد ہو رہے گا
اُفق پہ جب صبح کا کنارا
کسی کرن سے دہک اُٹھے گا
کہ ایک درماندہ راہرو کی
جبیں پہ شبنم کا ہاتھ چمکے

The desert has bared its human heart
which now caressed
by a dim white light
is longing for a drop of dew
to fall anywhere.

This burning moon is bound
to turn cold: it will turn cold
when on the horizon
the edge of morning
will suddenly catch fire,

ignited by some random ray,
and on the forehead
of some helpless, weary traveller
the dew will place
its shining hand.

*(Adapted from Faiz's Urdu translation of a poem by
Uljaz Omar Ali Suleiman, a renowned poet of Kazakhstan)*

لاؤ تو قتل نامہ مرا

سننے کو بھیڑ ہے سرِ محشر لگی ہوئی
تہمت تھی اسے عشق کی ہم پر لگی ہوئی

زندوں کے دم سے آتش نے کے بغیر بھی
ہے ہر کدے میں آگ برابر لگی ہوئی

آباد کر کے شہرِ خموشاں ہر ایک سو
کس کوچ میں ہے تیغِ ستمگر لگی ہوئی

آخر کو آج اپنے لہو پر ہوئی تمام
بازی میں اِن قاتل و خنجر لگی ہوئی

"لاؤ تو قتل نامہ مرا میں بھی دیکھ لوں
کس کس کی مُہر ہے سرِ محضر لگی ہوئی"

98

So Bring the Order for My Execution

The Day of Judgment is here.
A restless crowd has gathered all around the field.
This is the accusation: that I have loved you.

No wine is left in the taverns of this earth.
But those who swear by rapture,
this is their vigil:

they've made sure,
simply with a witnessing thirst,
that intoxication is not put out today.

In whose search is the swordsman now?
His blade red, he's just come from the City of Silence,
its people exiled or finished to the last.

The suspense that lasts between killers and weapons
as they gamble: who will die and whose turn is next?
That bet has now been placed on me.

So bring the order for my execution.
I must see with whose seals the margins are stamped,
recognize the signatures on the scroll.

تم ہی کہو کیا کرنا ہے

جب دُکھ کی ندیا میں ہم نے
بجوں کی ناؤ ڈالی تھی
تھا کتنا کس بل یا بنہوں میں
لہو میں کتنی لالی تھی
یوں لگتا تھا دو ہاتھ لگے
اور ناؤ پورم پار لگی
ایسا نہ ہوا، ہر دھارے میں
کچھ ان دیکھی منجدھاریں تھیں
کچھ ماجھی تھے انجان بہت
کچھ بے پرکھی پتواریں تھیں
اب جو بھی چاہو چھان کرو
اب جتنے چاہو دوکش دھرو
ندیا تو وہی ہے ناؤ وہی
اب تم ہی کہو کیا کرنا ہے
اب کیسے پار اترنا ہے

جب اپنی چھاتی میں ہم نے
اس دیس کے گھاؤ دیکھے تھے
تھا ویدوں پر روشواش بہت
اور یاد بہت سے نسخے تھے
یوں لگتا تھا بس کچھ دن میں
ساری پیتا کٹ جائے گی
اور سب گھاؤ بھر جائیں گے
ایسا نہ ہوا کہ روگ اپنے
کچھ اتنے ڈھیر پُرانے تھے
ویدان کی ٹوہ کو پا نہ سکے
اور ٹوٹکے سب بیکار گئے
اب جو بھی چاہو چھان کرو
اب چاہو جتنے دوکش دھرو
چھاتی تو وہی ہے گھاؤ وہی
اب تم ہی کہو کیا کرنا ہے
یہ گھاؤ کیسے بھرنا ہے

لندن شہر

100

You *Tell Us What to Do*

When we launched life
on the river of grief,
how vital were our arms, how ruby our blood.
With a few strokes, it seemed,
we would cross all pain,
we would soon disembark.
That didn't happen.
In the stillness of each wave we found invisible currents.
The boatmen, too, were unskilled,
their oars untested.
Investigate the matter as you will,
blame whomever, as much as you want,
but the river hasn't changed,
the raft is still the same.
Now *you* suggest what's to be done,
you tell us how to come ashore.

When we saw the wounds of our country
appear on our skins,
we believed each word of the healers.
Besides, we remembered so many cures,
it seemed at any moment
all troubles would end, each wound heal completely.
That didn't happen: our ailments
were so many, so deep within us
that all diagnoses proved false, each remedy useless.
Now do whatever, follow each clue,
accuse whomever, as much as you will,
our bodies are still the same,
our wounds still open.
Now tell us what we should do,
you tell us how to heal these wounds.

About the Translator

Agha Shahid Ali was born in New Delhi and raised in Kashmir. He has published several collections of poems including *The Half-Inch Himalayas*, *A Walk Through the Yellow Pages*, and *A Nostalgist's Map of America*, (forthcoming), as well as a scholarly work, *T.S. Eliot as Editor*. His poems, essays, translations and reviews have appeared in *Poetry*, *Paris Review*, *Chelsea*, *Grand Street*, *Yale Journal of Criticism*, *Denver Quarterly*, and other journals all over the world. Agha Shahid Ali teaches English and creative writing at Hamilton College.

The Peregrine Smith Poetry Series

Christopher Merrill, General Editor

Sequences, by Leslie Norris
Stopping By Home, by David Huddle
Daylight Savings, by Steven Bauer
The Ripening Light, by Lucile Adler
Chimera, by Carol Frost
Speaking in Tongues, by Maurya Simon
The Rebel's Silhouette, by Faiz Ahmed Faiz
   (translated by Agha Shahid Ali)